EASTLAKE CLEANERS WHEN QUALITY & PRICE COUNT
[A ROMANCE]

~ *Concrete Wolf* 2006 Editor's Choice Award

ALSO FROM CONCRETE WOLF
POETRY CHAPBOOK SERIES:

2001
The Grape Painter
by Lou Suarez

2002
The Tallahassee Letters
by Ryan G. Van Cleave

2003
Such Short Supply
by Michelle Brooks

2004
Squeezers
by Alison Pelegrin

2005
Special Two Chapbook Issue
Put Your Sorry Side Out
by Lois Marie Harrod
&
The Way Out West
by J.R. Thelin

2006
A Pilgrim's Guide To Chaos in the Heartland
by Jessica Goodfellow

Eastlake Cleaners When Quality & Price Count

[a romance]

Janet Norman Knox

Concrete Wolf **Poetry Chapbook Series**

Copyright © 2007 Janet Norman Knox

ISBN 978-0-9797137-0-5

Designed and composed in Arno Pro Opticals
at Hobblebush Books, Brookline, NH
(www.hobblebush.com)

Printed in Seattle, Washington, United States of America

All paintings by Tom Fehsenfeld, Eastlake Cleaners series
(encaustic, 4 by 6 feet)
Author's portrait on back cover by Jim Fagiolo, www.jimfagiolo.com

The author gratefully acknowledges *The Diagram*/New Michigan Press
("Instructions for Hard Cleaning", "Murmuration", "Believing in Birds", "A
Year Passes Like a Snowflake"), *Diner* ("Parking Lot's Wife"), *Crab Creek
Review* ("Da Vinci's Dragon in a Permian Tree"), *Arabesques* ("Thinking
of Lady With Ankh-Cross on Early Morning before Dry Cleaners Open"),
Art Access ("Pruned, It Will Grow Back" and "Double Paned Friendship"),
Seattle Woman ("When You Cannot See Your Child's Sun"), and *Red
Mountain Review* ("Follow the Bouncing Ball"), where first these poems
appeared.

Concrete Wolf Poetry Chapbook Series

CONCRETE WOLF
P.O. Box 788
Kirkland, Washington 98083-0788

www.ConcreteWolf.com
ConcreteWolf@yahoo.com

To my husband, Tom Fehsenfeld, and our children, Thane, Theo, and Xander. To poets Ilya Kaminsky, Lana Hechtman-Ayers, Elane Helmuth, Kelli Russell Agodon, Natasha Kochicheril Moni, Annette Spaulding-Convy, Jeannine Hall Gailey, Jenifer Browne Lawrence, Ronda Broatch, and Holly Hughes. To alpine women Barbara Trafton, Kayla Black, Sally Black, Barbara Zaroff, Anne Barker, Pamela Dharamsey Lee, Marcie Spahi, and Molly Knox.

Contents

When you drop off your order, a game of tag ensues

[a translator's note]

Your cleaner is it and counts then labels the shirts and skirts. She chases the alchemy of red wine stain, twenty incantations will fix a double crease. She finds a pressed clover ready or not so lucky left in pocket and with one finger, she touches base. Your cleaner safety-pins a tag and seeks missing buttons or tears. Run and hide. Droplets on her brow, her faraway eyes say homefree. You are it as you pick up a crisp skin wrapped in plastic, but who has won?

INSTRUCTIONS FOR HARD CLEANING

Black letters proclaim
things that are hard
to clean. *Sleeping Bags Rugs*
not your normal Monday washing, not

your sheets, not towels, the weight
of wet beyond the scale of small
to large to modest loads.
Blankets Leathers

Wedding Gowns cool
after a long honey
stain to remove, to shuffle away
between sheets of tissue to dry
a salty eye for a child

to grow into. *Comforters*
promise olamic sleep,
cushion the cleaning,
Pillows the head
held high over spit
of starch. *Down*

Garments like wearing *Pillows*
the landings in an icy
marriage. *Drapes* to cloak
reason to come *When*
Quality & Price Count.
Repellents. We do not agree.

Come to *Eastlake Cleaners*
to be taught to love
city birds in city
trees, grain cast
in wind, we will fly
by the window
and we will learn.

Parking Lot's Wife

She is thwacking rugs, doormat-
sized in shades of tweed to hide the
dirt. She smacks them against the
concrete column in the parking lot
at *Eastlake Cleaners When Quality
& Price Count*. A stiff rug, a firm
grasp, a wide swing, slap against the
pillar, freshly painted by a man who
toiled for days, never took a break
to trace the curl of wind in birches.
He masked every corner of brick,
each window ledge. He painted
around and around pillars, nine
lives of them dizzy with devotion.
She slips her hands in pockets, leans
against a pillar, gazes brazenly back
at fall leaves quivering, small flames.
Reflecting a life she left, her eyes
brim with brine. She has waited
since she was six in Seoul for the
dragon to rise from the lake and
now it laces red breath though leaves.

Murmuration

Bird warbled to bird, overheard,
eavesdropped on the party line, wind whistling
poles crackling Alexander
Graham Bell.

Now twenty pairs
of claws clench
the telephone wire. Beaks preen.
Wings stretch iridescence, await

Joo-Eun, *Silver Pearl*
to finish her afternoon
cleaning.

She will dust the parking lot with gilded grain. Here

at the door to *Eastlake*
Cleaners When Quality & Price
Count, she coaxes crumbs to English Sparrows.
She whispers Korean vo-

wels like pearls.
They understand as one
wisdom, syllables
silver and ringing.

She Scatters a Fistful of Rice, Knowing Full Well the Grain Will Not Swell in Their Gullets

There, she chased migrating geese from the rice crop, a sign
of famine. She throws a handful now to keep

the crop full, to fuel a cold day. She hears that brides
shower in rice here. When she wed, she fed

jujubes like sweet children
to her mother-in-law's downcast eyes.

Her groom dowered a goose,
a sign of fidelity. *Comforters*

Wedding Gowns, Drapes—signs of the faithful
unsoiling at *Eastlake Cleaners*, a loyal goose

foraging in rice fields, fattening
before winter's flight, cleaning

to do, giving the goose, mating
for life, feeding the rice.

Da Vinci's Dragon in a Permian Tree

You ask whether I'm stalking
The Lady of the Lake, The Lady

of Eastlake Cleaners. Whether I am a lowly
lizard, one Leonardo

made dragon by knotting tiny wings
across its shoulders, silk and balsa,

thread and wax, tied in a bow, a gift
to be opened in flight.

* * *

Stunted trees, grandmothers
clutch the trampled earth.

They gaze at sky, wishing for wings
to lift rooted feet. Whether plastic bags

caught in twigs, fluttering a friendly
wave, will lift a tree in air. *Gingko,*

we guess, small fans of modesty,
memory of Permian dragons

folded into pleats of bark.

* * *

Whether breath melts icicles, swords
on Maidenhair.

Whether a tree frees to fly.

Eyes On Us

She knows where dragons live.
Some migratory, others resident.

She visits their nests, watches.
One fledgling found a mate, lives at the south end
          of the island. She calls rounds
of sound, like lobbing softballs
through fog, a high arch.
       Wait. Stand still. Suit of night.

       Another call, a wide spin,
              Mezzo Soprano with Frisbee.
              It may take several minutes to hear

a response, if at all,
(dragons are not active in rain or thick fog. They huddle,
wrapped in wings.)

She hears a response. Patient. Distant.
There.

I call you, husband. Listen, my eyes become accustomed. I will not
       need light.

The dragon may perch on a low branch,
fifteen feet above our heads. Eyes on us
       peering at a live night thing.

Way of Pollen

We look at the Way and it is invisible.
—LAO TSU

I.
Asian Pears

Planted together, early blooming
Ya Li and Tsu Li, are placed
for cross pollination to bear full crops
of Asian pears, seed carried
on feet of bees.

II.
Solitary Bees

Solitary bees—
working alone, preferring
not hives, not
queens, cities of mason bees
in ground or wood, a drop of nectar
for our larvae. Ya Li and Tsu Li
bloom and we, we light from pear blossom to pear

III.
Workers

blossom. At computer, at cleaning,
a grain of pollen to feed our young
thoughts. Through branches, Ya Li
and Tsu Li share said and unsaid, share divining sky.

PRUNED, IT WILL GROW BACK

Succisa virescit
—BENEDICTINE MOTTO

Walking Eastlake,
its thick trunk turning

a lesson of will, a deep
    purple not pruned or bound bonsai.

Never a sharp steel blade.

        The oldest lilac
        tortes sweetly, tea cake toward
        an eastern sun, a wind
        off the lake tousles

Erika turning a bed
            perennial, hard
            at work, sleeves rolled, digging
            the loam of thought. She lived the first
green shoots of persecution, her father, a doctor
                in Berlin.

Her neighbor cut the limbs of the tree that grew into his yard so he would
    not be infected.

Let your lilac grow.
Let it reach into my
yard, balm of unkindest
cut, growing.

We search each others' eyes, hers violet, the color of will, the color of her
    tattoo, this fading.

THE TREES ARE FULL OF ASIAN PEARS—GOLDFINCHES DULLED BY FALL, OCHRE AND BRASS, THEY WORK EACH BRANCH.

An old Korean variety, Okusankichi,
   ripens in October and stores well,
   fruit borne on two-year-old spurs.
    Older wood give smaller fruit.

She limps, a tired leg, old wood.
    She bows to the pigeon that struts
    into *Eastlake Cleaners*, the door ajar,
     even in frost, to let out fumes.

The first to flower are fragile,
    fruit is bronze to russet, oblong.
   At harvest, its flavor is fair
   but sweetens in storage.

At the door, finches swarm her, flush
    of feather, pillow of winged pears
    lift her in flight. She takes on light
    like pear blossoms at night
    petal cups full with white.

Pre-treatment [The wet, the dry, the ugly]

[further translation needed]

Your cleaner looks at your clothes, mutters tsk-tsk, treats the stain with care. Catch the stain early. Apply water for wet stains (water-based, full of bean soup or mango juice) and solvent for dry stains (greasy or oily like peanut butter). Tap and blot both sides of the fabric with a soft cloth so the stain bleeds into the cloth. If you don't know what to do when stained, play tag with your cleaner.

We see the clothes loaded, rotating in a perforated basket, a spray of solvent. The dirty solvent is pumped through a filter clear of dirt. Clothes drop and pound against baffles. Drycleaning the obvious, we are baffled.

ABSTRACT: Complete blindness for 9 days with bright phosphenes and pain on eye rotation. It takes months to recover only central vision.

CONCLUSION: Although ambient concentrations of perchloroethylene are within normal limits, we measure five-fold increases in vapors emitted when ironing freshly dry-cleaned fabrics. We suggest that inhalation of perchloroethylene vapors is the cause of this case of ocular nerve toxicity. We have seen too much. We do not want to be it.

Believing in Birds

In plainword, let's run through that again—she steps out

of *Eastlake Cleaners* and is swarmed
by a plural of birds, a charm
of finches.

This is not Hitchcock, no flights of fancy. This is not a thaumaturgy.
This is not
          an evangelist's tent.

A halo of wing surrounds
a woman who is not stunned, smiles,
calmly lifts her arms, conducting

a feathered symphony. Shall I report this to the Department

of Miracle Control, tie small prayers
          on gingko branches? Shall I build altars
          in the parking lot and shower

them with blossoms? Should we canonize her for gifts to lowly
workers who do not sing?

We hear them crying
the way they do when they are ready
          to settle for the night.

Thinking of Lady with Ankh-Cross in Early Morning before Dry Cleaners Open

Antinoopolis, c. 193–235 A.D.

From where you lie, a canvas
on a far wall glows ochre—
Fayum painters blend fleshtone

from charcoal, rust hematite, yellow earth,
chalk, wine dregs dried to indigo.
As wax cools, a chill hovers.

Ptolemy rulers line temple walls, shroud
those they portray. The Lady
holds the Ankh-Cross in her left hand,

displays her right palm, making a sign—
Fare well or *Stay there*.
She may pull you from dead

middle of the lake,
back arching, muscles taut,
you hear a lute string plucked.

Waiting for Dragons

We do not use dry cleaners
ourselves, wearing clothes
that drip dry, we cultivate
wrinkles.

* * *

We watch droplets
condense from a vent pipe
around back, bracketed
to the outside wall, drop

* * *

by drop, a slow release
each barely detected
but together so clean.
So neat. So pressed. So

* * *

they infiltrate a secret
seam running from Eastlake
to Lake Union where the dragon
waits to one day
      rise in the air.

* * *

We will not know at first
what we are seeing, a flash
of light, a blink
of eye. Some will say

they heard the egress of egret or heron.

* * *

Those who work inside
keep the door ajar, escaping
fumes welcome fresh air.
We want them to breathe,

their lungs a pink clutch
of balloons to celebrate
the flush of birds, the gilding
    of Asian pears, the breath of dragons.

Guardian Angel Making the Rounds

Eddie counts
       the alleys of Eastlake—curbs

to trip, slabs
of concrete
       rootless serpents

writhing underground.
He brims
       with suggestion,

mostly precautionary. *Better not*

hang around here
after dinner. Your pea
patch is catching
weeds.

He doesn't want everyone
to get hurt. He overlooks
       Eastlake Cleaners, figures

they can take care
of themselves. Eddie
       has no need

for creases. Except his brow.
He has lost
       some weight,

got a new jaw,
pair of jeans,
       a smaller waist

number on the back
label.

EASTLAKE AVENUE,
A TIDAL CREEK

We commute
from pillow
to hard work,
sidewalking.
Shopping cart
barges block
our sight
from the
pilot house.
We reverse
the engines,
but momen-
tum carries
us. We pour
salt water
from boot
to boot,
not full.
A salt
wedge
weighting
back a
fresh drink,
parched,
buoyed down
the Eastlake, a
long Nile,   Amazon,
Mississippi   the   slowing
delta dropping   sediment,   gravid
hope, flowing   change, birth   ing sea.

Eastlake lies

on her side, a worthy nude round in
spots, lean and sinew so new, yet
wizened, her lying in wait moist with
waterfall wishing above her, I-5 a canopy,
her anklets and toe rings—the works,
alluring. A siren wails, beckons kayakers
or weekend sailors luffing from the
Wooden Boat Center across Lake Union.
She is inclined to accept it all as is, as
truth in the shallows of the lake,
sprawling west, squinting into a sugar
mile over plain water. East late the wee
hours of the 4th, we criss cross her
ravaged thigh, spent gown stained and
heaped to heft up the hill to *Eastlake
Cleaners When* pressed and folded until
the next fest
and its fire
works.

I Will Make It All Up

What will I say when I walk in the door,
        I have no excuse to walk through
        the door.

I will make it all up, half-
        truth, a fullstain
        on my shirt, a sip,
        slip of sauce at Hiroshi's Sushi
        next door. A slurp
        of Udon wriggling like worm

sends me splattered with drips to rush through the door,
        always ajar where I point
        and plead *Help*. How will I say
        I witness her marvel
        at finch at leaf?

Will I ask after pigeons, compliment courage
        will I ask *do you like it here*?
        Eastlake Cleaners. It must be hard

cleaning.

Finishing

Pressing, folding, packaging, and other tied up in a bow touches.
We are unburdened. The dry cleaners bestows gifts without wait.
The dragon appears on the columns to signify an understanding.
Les colonnes sur lesquelles, on aperçoit le Dragon représentant
symboliquement la reconnaissance de tous les secrets. Blinding-
white button-downs, paid in gold each hour stand stiff like pillars
to ward off wrinkles, stuck with pins, being it.

    The finish is touched and tarnished.

A YEAR PASSES LIKE A SNOWFLAKE

falling into a lake a moment
intricate
        white
              dissolved

(waiting for moon)

to join thousands of liquid years
glacier lake made pure

(to rise through tree trunks)

by snowflake each your face
at the edge of vision lace repeating

(moon in the wrong part of sky)

itself tatted by hand every expression
crystalline perfection

(where it has never been before)

your face on my skin melts a year
passes like a snowflake

When You Cannot See Your Child's Sun*

These are small things, the button
down collar, the crease
in pants. The firm

requirements of work, lips pressed
tight against chest
like a hand

of cards. This is how
you gambled, crossed an East Sea on a deck
        of cards, to house the dry

cleaner where your daughter
must do homework.
        Open the door

        a thin crack—
        a flash of steam a sting
of eyes a scald of lungs—exhausted

        out a vent, and when the wind
rises, a solvent mist. Look
                at the wind rose,

        pink petals show
        where the wind blows.
The wind will rouse.

---

* The loss of blue-yellow color vision has been found in studies of dry cleaner health.
The exact pathogenic mechanism of the impairment is still unclear. An irreversible
PCE-related color-vision loss suggests anatomical damage to the cones, whereas
reversibility may be related to cone or neurotransmitter function.

Small things—ironing
in a PCE cloud, your child coloring.
When you cannot see

a child's sun, a child's sea,
it is then that you see
it is not such a small thing—

the seeing of yellow the seeing of blue   seeing red—
fist tight against your chest,
a rose floating in a gasp of wind.

Protected by the Wrath of Gwenhwyfar

She is our Korean lady
of the court, feudal Asian,
black lines painted on a powdered brow.

The drama is clear—
Kurosawa's Ran is King Lear,
she is our Guinevere: cultures steep in pots
of Woojeon and Earl Grey.

We find her Woojeon,
Before the Rains,
pacing the sidewalk.

She marches the castle keep clad, glad in gold
and miniver. She vows
to pick early leaves before the rains, scarce

but worth the care. Fingers
gather leaves, twist, dry,
imbue with hot rain to brew the richest tea. *Quality
& Price Count*. Rare
but worthy, she reminds us not to miss
the leaves unfurling flags of small surrender.

She surveys the realm,
her face reflecting light
in which we see

ourselves. All is well
in Camelot's parking lot.

The Dancer Iridescent

It was just a parking lot
before she entered, pavement
of paradise, puddle of sheen.

Now it lights up like a stage
as she appears. There are no motion
detectors. Every step choreographed, a sweep
of skirt, hands punctuate apron pockets.

Her scenery is curbs, lines of parking spots. They
divine space, an abstract geometry, masking
tape Xes glow in blackout.

She finds her position
and the lights fade up, skirt stretched across a wide plié.
She curls an arm around a column, lunges into tarmac, lit by follow
spot, whistles to finches, cheeks beam.

As she exits, cars
coast in, filling space between parallel lines, she exists.

PREVALENT WIND

Wind coming or going, passing
        through our skin.

    Listen, whisked
        in gust, she is gone—

    another cleaners, the other
        side of Lake Union, another

     Pacific shore, she crossed

    the Pretty River on a whisper
        of better

     life humming a tune.

     She [will not take the wind out]

[will not trade her] is wind.
      [The wind is not ill.]

     She [is not against the wind]

will not cool the thermal
on which we rise.

DOUBLE PANED FRIENDSHIP

You ask, my friend, am I spying
on the *Eastlake Cleaners* Lady
through my low-E window.

Is it wrong to make friends
through double paned windows,
cross oceans of asphalt?

Is it eaves-eyeing, nosy parker
of the parking lot, shall we mind our own
business when we are at work?

Windows provide light and ventilation.
If they choose, they open. The pane
of friendship. Who has not

breathed the desperate fumes
of a window stuck shut,
a high-rise faulty design?

We classify them by how they open
and close. Some friends are double-hung, double
indemnity. Some are casement, all

or nothing, an open and painted-shut case.
We yawn at all the friends. Always ajar,
she steps out the door (no more will I take you to the cleaners,

my friend, I open the window and let you in) she steps
out of the door, smiles at the sky
at me at my computer through

two layers of glass,
hermetically-sealed, we emit
understanding. Of light. An exchange.

Chartreuse Leaves

Jules fills mailboxes, (vatic)
about the sendings

and leavings of Eastlake, gossip
or glue (static). He will know if I ask the name

of the tree. *Gingko, Maidenhair* (didactic). Her name—
does not know. When she first came *When*

Quality & Price Count
the leaves oranged

in blush or fervor. Now past
naked boughs, past bud, past new

leaf, I cannot see past
the block of parking lot.

Past mailboxes filled with love
letters, poetry of rejection.

Fill my eyes, fan leaves,
so that I might not see her stencil

cut shadow. Strip mall in chill
spring, sun on damp blacktop, (*you will hear*

a rushing in your ears)
(emphatic), a steam rises.

ALL HER NAMES

I am coming clean. You ask
whether I know her by name.

By speaking the tongue
of birds, her name is Joo-Eun, *Silver Pearl*, trills and coos.

By thwacking rugs her name
is Hea Yong, *Grace Courage*, her arms able.

She shies not from the hard
grasp of work. By casting of grain

her name is Kyung Soon, *Gentle Honor*.
By her visage like moon that knows

her way across Ha-neul, *Sky*, in egg blue
of day, a face full

of Hyun Bae, *Inspired Wisdom*.
You ask how I dreamt

her dreams, how I sow her seeds,
how I understand

her words, how
I go bird

nesting, eggs of song birds, clean
blueness in the shadows of nests,

concealed from Steller's
Jays and small, winged dragons.

FOLLOW THE BOUNCING BALL

Shuang Ying zips into *Eastlake Cleaners*
When Quality & Price Count.
The whites of four furred feet
and her sneakers catch
my eye like bouncing
balls in a sing-along of *This Land*
Is Your Land. They rebound
in cheerful arches from word
to word along the refrain.
She could be you and she is

for an instant and then
she isn't. The door swings open
and she reappears, her dog
scurrying to the next sniff
in a dot-to-dot of smell,
until it loops back to number
one. Home. She is a slight

variation of you, wearing black
with white accents, little dog pulling
her faster down a sidewalk,
her muscles tense against a leash,
a line taut between white nose of dog
and heels leaning back, dug

into concrete. Across the land,
women are pulled home
by thoughts of cleaning or cooking
rice, corn, rye, wheat,
grains of peace. We could
be them and we are.

Reconcile: After Laundry Pick-up

*W*hat is left of Eastlake Cleaners When discarded hangers clang for order or bird seed demanding grains of truth cast in wind raining down to feed a hungry crawl? How do we make change as a tangle of hangers sweeps from the tarmac, taking flight? How do they turn as one, a dip of wing, a twist, a hook? They hover waiting for us to figure it out, make peace, or follow. Flapping, treading air, the tips of their wings trace infinity signs as they rise. ⤎

About the Author

JANET NORMAN KNOX's poems have been nominated for the Pushcart Prize and have appeared in journals such as *Crab Creek Review, Rhino, Diner, Seattle Review, Adirondack Review, Tattoo Highway, Poetry Southeast, Cranky Literary Journal, Red Mountain Review,* and *Diagram.* She was a 2007 finalist for the Discovery/The Nation award.